HOW TO CREATE MACHINE SUPERINTELLIGENCE

A Quick Journey through Classical/Quantum Computing, Artificial Intelligence, Machine Learning, and Neural Networks.

SECOND EDITION

Artem Kovera

How to Create Machine Superintelligence: A Quick Journey through Classical/Quantum Computing, Artificial Intelligence, Machine Learning, and Neural Networks (Second Edition)

Copyright © 2018, 2021 by Artem Kovera

ISBN-13: 978-1986641234

ISBN-10: 1986641236

Table of Contents

"The first ultraintelligent machine is the last invention that man need ever make" I.J. Good, 1965

To the memory of professor Yuriy Syvolap

Introduction

Even though some occasional recessions and even depressions occur, in general, the history of mankind is a story of steady development. The main source of human development is the total human intelligence and information that is available to it. Obviously, mankind would not have been able, for example, to switch from hunting and gathering to agriculture and then to the industrial revolution if people had not been smart enough. We can say that intelligence is the resource that allows us to take advantage of all other resources.

Arguably, the complexity of the human brain makes us the special species on Earth, at least in terms of intellectual capabilities. Even some of the ancients believed that people are similar to animals in the way our bodies function and similar to gods in the way our minds function. We should not take it literally, of course, but this metaphorical notion means that the possession of the mind is the most valuable human characteristic.

In the last decade, many impressive technological achievements in artificial intelligence emerged, which had long been considered intractable for computers, for example, many types of pattern recognition and even pattern generation. These achievements are primarily based on the progress in artificial neural networks with multiple hidden layers, so-called deep neural networks. Today we use applications incorporating deep neural networks on a daily basis even without fully realizing it.

Today, more and more people are getting obsessed with the idea of *artificial general intelligence*, which someday may become able to accurately mimic human behavior and mental processes such as creativity and reasoning, so it would be very hard to tell the differences between humans and computers. Furthermore, machines may become much smarter than humans.

The reason for being deeply interested in artificial general intelligence is not only humans' inherent curiosity and imagination. Everyone understands that this is an extremely powerful technology, which can radically change our lives for good.

However, many computer scientists believe that we are still far away from creating really intelligent machines. They say that, probably, even human-level artificial general intelligence is still decades away, but it is also possible that some crucial breakthroughs for building AGI may occur very shortly.

The adoption of new technologies has been becoming increasingly faster over the course of the industrial era. So, we can expect the upcoming technological breakthroughs to be adopted and integrated into massive production even faster. When created, artificial general intelligence may irreversibly impact the whole human society in a very short term.

Imagine what an astonishing effect could happen if we combined profound human natural creativity with computers' numerical and logical capabilities. Probably, the corporations and nations that will use this technology first will immensely benefit from it.

In this synopsis, I will try to give a gentle and math-free introduction to artificial intelligence and related subjects such as deep learning and quantum computations with respect to the latest technologies written for people who do not necessarily have a background in computer science, mathematics, or engineering.

Recent advances in artificial intelligence have been overhyped many times by media. In this short book, we will discuss whether and how information technologies such as machine learning algorithms and deep artificial neural networks, in particular, may potentially lead to creating artificial general intelligence.

Intelligence as a Form of Information Processing

As, perhaps, all abstract concepts and ideas – such as love, freedom, consciousness – the term intelligence is not very well defined and even understood. Different thinkers suggest different definitions. These definitions put emphasis on different aspects of intelligence. According to one of those definitions, intelligence is the ability to solve problems using limited resources.

Not surprisingly, the term superintelligence is also quite vague. By convention, superintelligence is a type of intelligence that vastly more powerful than any natural human intelligence. In this book, I also hold to this definition of superintelligence.

We can think of intelligence as a microcosm that abstracts the macrocosm. Intelligence includes many components, but it's widely accepted that the prime function of intelligence is modeling the world in order to predict unknown things from something that is already known, for example, the future from the past or present. It is believed that the ability to predict everything from everything, of course, with some probability, is a key characteristic of intelligence. The process of prediction, I view through the lens of information processing.

Information is one of the universal properties, and all physical objects in the universe process information. From the point of view of theoretical computer science, information processing is a computation, and it is a good idea to clarify what in principle can be computed.

In order to solve a problem using a computer, a machine has to be supplied with an algorithm. An algorithm is basically a sequence of certain instructions. Different algorithms may require different numbers of steps and be more or less simple or extremely complex.

In the early twentieth century, many brilliant mathematicians, including the famous German mathematician and logician David Hilbert, worked on the logical basis of mathematics. In 1928, he formulated a problem, known under its rather intimidating German name *Entscheidungsproblem,* which means the decision problem. This problem asks whether there exists a definite method that can prove whether any logical statement is true.

In 1936, Alan Turing invented an abstract model of computation, which later became known as a Turing machine, capable of performing all possible algorithms. The Turing machine is a model of modern computers. Whatever we can do on a computer, we can also do using Turing's computational model. With the help of his abstract machine, Turing resolved the *Entscheidungsproblem* and showed that there is no method to prove all logical statements. Turing achieved this result by describing the *halting problem*. He proved that there is no universal algorithm to show whether the execution of a given program will terminate on any given input of data.

Right before Alan Turing discovered his abstract machine, the American mathematician Alonzo Church had also significantly contributed to the computability theory by creating a method for defining functions called lambda calculus and resolved the *Entscheidungsproblem* independently from Turing.

The *Church–Turing thesis* states that no computer can solve any problems which cannot be solved by Turing's machine. The Turing machine cannot solve all the problems; therefore, any physical computer cannot solve all the problems either, even if it had unlimited computational resources.

There is an opinion that if the problems that cannot be solved on computers exist, artificial general intelligence implemented in computer systems cannot be built. However, the halting problem can be applied not only to computers but also to all information-processing systems, including the human mind, because any intelligence is a sophisticated form of information processing.

It is interesting that some great philosophers had been thinking about the limitations of our intelligence long before the amazing mathematical discoveries of the first half of the 20th century. For example, the father of German classical philosophy Immanuel Kant put forward the idea that the human mind cannot fully contemplate itself as a mind. Maybe, this example shows that sometimes philosophy can come to the objective truth before science or at least provide science with valuable ideas.

Another consequence of the halting problem is that a universal debugger for computer programs cannot exist. Moreover, the halting problem also has a profound philosophical consequence: no one agent can know for certain its future actions.

In addition to the halting problem, the universal unpredictability has two other prerequisites. The first one is quantum mechanical uncertainty. Heisenberg's uncertainty principle states that we cannot exactly know both the velocity and position of any particle at the same time. At the most fundamental level of reality, all physical processes are deeply probabilistic. At a macroscopic level, however, myriads of microscopic processes average out in some sense, so the overall macroscopic behavior gets much more deterministic. But some inherent unpredictability of the world still remains even at a macroscopic scale.

Another prerequisite of unpredictability is the fact that all objects are influenced by all other objects in the universe. So, in order to know something for sure, we must know the precise state of the rest of the universe. But to know the precise state of the universe we should at least have a computer with a memory the size of the universe plus the memory itself, which is logically impossible.

I suppose that these three sources of unpredictability, like everything in the universe, are deeply interconnected, and they may be the derivatives of one universal law of unpredictability.

Because of this intrinsic unpredictable nature of reality, any information-processing system including any superintelligence cannot create a completely precise model of the world and predict the future with complete accuracy. Or put more simply, everyone, including superintelligence, makes mistakes. In fact, any model is an approximation. Moreover, in modeling nonlinear systems, even extremely small errors at the beginning can yield dramatically large errors at the end. This gives rise to a well-known butterfly effect.

Here we should mention that because of constant Brownian motion, different particles or molecules in the brain like neurotransmitters move in an intrinsically unpredictable fashion. I don't think that in order to build machine superintelligence we should create an artificial intelligence system which will copy this natural approach for the reason that such an unpredictable system would be immensely difficult for us to control.

Everything *algorithmically computable* can be solved by a Turing machine, and any ordinary computer, even the simplest one, can perform any algorithm, which means that computers are universal. Though implementing some algorithms may take an unreasonably long time and anyone doesn't know in advance with 100% certainty whether the implementation of an algorithm stops and gives any output if this implementation hasn't been done before. Another important conclusion is that a given computer can simulate any information-processing system. Therefore, if intelligence is a product of an information-processing system, it can be simulated on computers.

Another important concept is that the same information can be supplied to different algorithms which will give different outputs. This observation refers to the concept of *meaning*. The same information can mean different things to different types of intelligence.

All algorithmically-solvable problems can be divided into several major classes based on their computational complexity. There are problems which are very easily solvable on a computer, but there are also increasingly difficult ones because solving different computational problems may require intrinsically different amounts of computational resources.

Under the computational resources, computer scientists typically mean, first of all, the number of elementary steps of an algorithm or program execution, and the amount of computer memory to solve a problem. It is not surprising that the computational resources are always limited. The amount of computational work varies depending on the scale of input data. The more input data, the more computational resources are needed.

The majority of the algorithms executed on computers belong to the class P of computational problems. Such algorithms can be executed in polynomial time – time upper bounded by a polynomial expression in the size of the input for the algorithm. These algorithms can be efficiently implemented on computers. The class P lies within the class NP.

The problems within the class NP that do not belong to the class P are not efficiently solvable on computers, even though their solutions can be efficiently verified. For these problems, algorithm time execution increases very quickly (exponentially) as the input data size grows. For example, for an algorithm of the time complexity

10^x, if an input data size $x = 2$ requires 100 steps to complete, an input data size $x = 3$ will require 1000 steps, and an input data size $x = 4$ will require 10000 steps. These problems are called *NP problems*. For instance, factoring numbers is one example of NP problems. If we know a solution to any NP problem, we can verify this solution in polynomial time. Solving these problems often requires using a brute-force search through all possible solutions to a given problem. Even though such problems can be solved by a computer in principal, they may, and most often, require unreasonable time and therefore are considered to be intrinsically difficult or intractable.

The hardest NP problems are called *NP-complete* problems. Actually, there are plenty of NP-complete problems. If a program that could solve any NP-complete in polynomial time were found, any NP problem could be solved in polynomial time, and it would mean that P=NP. We should also mention that NP-complete problems are not the hardest among all possible computational problems; for some problems, we cannot even verify the answers in reasonable (polynomial) time.

It had long been thought that nature can somehow solve NP-complete problems in the process of protein folding. Most proteins in biological organisms fold or, in other words, acquire their 3-dimensional structure almost instantaneously. At the same time, it's known that a 3-dimensional structure is stable in a molecule conformation with the lowest free energy, and the number of different conformations is tremendously large (this number is once estimated 10^{143} for a middle-sized protein molecule, and this number grows exponentially with the size of the molecule). In order to find the conformation with the lowest free energy, a protein molecule has to search through all possible conformations, but this search must take an unreasonably long time. This is known as Levinthal's paradox. However, it turned out later that as a result of the enormous amount of selection pressure during the evolution process, the majority of proteins in biological organisms actually acquire their 3-dimensional structures not with the lowest free energy, but rather with a local minimum of free energy. Because of this, the process of protein folding in biological organisms usually runs very quickly. Perhaps, natural intelligence can use similar approaches in order to find some not perfect but reasonably appropriate solutions to some NP or NP-complete problems.

I should mention that in addition to P, NP, and NP-complete problems, there are also computational problems that can be solved *probabilistically* in polynomial time; this class is called BPP, and it may very likely be larger than P. It's thought by some experts that BPP represents all the problems which can be efficiently solved by natural or artificial intelligences.

It has not yet been formally proved, though, that there are no algorithms executed in polynomial time for NP problems. Maybe, such algorithms exist, but they haven't yet been discovered. If all NP problems belong to the P class, many problems that computer scientists have long struggled with are easy for computers to solve. However, the majority of experts in this field think that tractable in reasonable time algorithms do not exist for NP problems, and the formal proof for this only remains to be discovered, which is, by the way, one of the greatest unsolved mathematical challenges.

Classical Computing

In 1854, George Boole published *An Investigation of the Laws of Thought*, where he showed that any logical statements, including complex mathematical calculations, can be built by using three basic logic operations or gates: NOT, AND, and OR. Microprocessors in electronic computers implement various logical expressions using these gates.

A core component of every digital electronic computer is a central processing unit (CPU), which is basically a microprocessor. Simply put, a microprocessor is one or several integrated circuits. Each integrated circuit is a silicon plate with a certain number of transistors etched on it. A transistor can be interpreted as an electric switch. Most logic gates are composed of several transistors. Nowadays, advanced processors contain several billions of transistors.

Microprocessors are not only the components of personal computers. Now they are almost ubiquitous in our environment and scattered in a wide variety of devices from home appliances to ultra-sophisticated supercomputers.

As we have just seen, electronic computers are universal; that is, in principle, all algorithmically solvable problems can be worked out on any type of computer. However, different hardware architecture performs different tasks with varied efficiency. For example, graphical cards (GPUs) are such types of microprocessors that have been specifically designed for efficient graphical processing; a CPU can also process visual graphics, but a GPU does it better.

Each microprocessor has a defined set of elementary instructions that it can implement. There are arithmetic, logic, and control instructions. Everything that the processor does, no matter how complex the computations are, boils down to implementing these atomic instructions. Different instructions may require different execution times. For example, a single summation instruction may require only one clock cycle, whereas a single division instruction may require 20 or even 30 cycles. There is a term *instruction set architecture* (ISA). A laptop or desktop computer with a modern Intel or AMD processor inside most likely has a more complex ISA with more instructions available than a processor in a smartphone, not to mention a microcontroller in some piece of consumer electronics equipment, but all these microprocessors are universal in a sense that they can implement any computations if given an appropriate amount of resources.

It also worth knowing, especially for a programmer, that even processors with large and complex instruction sets do not have dedicated elementary instructions for some mathematical operations such as differentiation or integration. For this reason, in software, these operations are implemented by iteratively using a large number of simple arithmetic instructions like division and subtraction, but the solutions become approximate with some degree of precision. Moreover, due to the finite amount of computer memory and for efficiency reasons, real numbers in computers are also often represented approximately. In one of the following chapters, you will see that numerical differentiation is the backbone of the algorithm for training artificial neural networks.

The more transistors, the more logic gates a microprocessor has, and the more computing power can be generated out of it. The miniaturization of circuit components means that the electrons have less distance to travel inside the circuits, making the circuits run faster. Having a greater number of transistors enables making individual operations of a processor more complex. Additionally, the smaller the size of circuit components, the less heat they dissipate and faster can be made to run, which increases the clock speed of the processor.

However, at some point, the speed cannot be substantially increased even if the miniaturization continues. Some physical properties impose limitations for increasing the speed at which silicon microprocessors can execute instructions working reliably. And manufacturers have already pretty much reached these limits. From the 2000s, the clock speed has been growing much slower than in the several previous decades.

The number of transistors per square inch on integrated circuits has steadily doubled about every eighteen months, almost up to the present time - this pattern is known as Moore's law. The whole electronics industry has been greatly influenced by Moore's law, and perhaps most advantages in this industry hinge on this law.

Obviously, transistors cannot be shrunk to infinitesimally small dimensions. There are certain fundamental barriers to the minimum size of a transistor. Moore's law has already considerably slowed down, and some experts in this field say that the end of integrated circuit components' miniaturization is already in sight.

Does this mean that computing power will not be increasing any longer? There are some reasons to be optimistic about the growth of total computational power available to mankind in the future.

First of all, even though Moore's law has slowed down, it still continues. Secondly, the production of microprocessors will certainly continue, and therefore there will be more and more computer power in use around the world. Moreover, the manufacturing of integrated circuits is getting cheaper with new technologies.

Parallel computing is now a very important trend in the computer industry. This type of computing uses multiple processing elements running simultaneously to solve computational tasks. In this case, a computational problem is broken down into multiple components which are processed in parallel. Some computational problems, however, are inherently serial and cannot be converted into parallel operations. But many other computational problems, including many ones in artificial intelligence, can be significantly speed up using parallel computing.

The majority of CPUs are already multicore, which means that the CPUs consist of several computational units that can solve computational problems in parallel. The smaller the transistors, the more cores can be built on a single chip. There are many other classes of parallel computing, for example, distributed computing, and computing on graphics processing units (GPUs).

GPUs may have thousands of arithmetic-logic units and can simultaneously perform thousands of operations. GPUs are especially good at matrix operations, and many types of machine learning work very well on GPUs.

Distributed computing is an important type of parallel computing. In distributed computing, computational problems are broken down and distributed among many individual computers. The internet and other networks allow obtaining massive parallelization, so great results can be achieved by using this method. Nowadays, many computational tasks are carried out in this way.

Probably, the simplest example of distributed computing is online multiplayer games. In this case, part of the computations is performed on the server and another part of the computations is performed on multiple gamers' computers. This example may seem trivial, but actually, it is not. Also, giant websites, which constantly process large amounts of data, like Google or Facebook can be examples of distributed computing.

Distributed computing has many other even more intricate and computationally-intensive forms. For example, Folding@home is a distributed computing project aimed to discover 3-d structures of certain protein macromolecules, which can be then used to produce new drugs, for example.

Not surprisingly, distributed computing is also widely applied in the field of applied artificial intelligence. For instance, big data analysis is often implemented using various distributed computing frameworks.

However, distributed computing has quite a number of disadvantages. First of all, in distributed computing, different computers have to extensively communicate with each other. The speed of this communication is relatively low and often slows down the computations substantially. Another downside of distributed computing is decreased reliability: when you have thousands of computers, chances are that at least one of them or some part of the network that connects the computers is broken, which may compromise the overall system in some variations of distributed computing. However, in many other situations, distributed computer systems may be much more reliable than their single-computer counterparts. Another important downside of distributed computing, which probably causes most problems in practice, is that different computers are not synchronized, so it is often very difficult to organize in the right way the entire process of computations distributed over multiple computers.

Another class of computing that harnesses computational parallelism is supercomputing, also known as high-performance computing (HPC). Clearly, supercomputing deals with solving very hard computational problems. There are several general variations of HPC architecture. A typical supercomputer consists of a large number of CPUs or GPUs working together on the same computational problem. Interestingly, the computational capabilities of HPC have been growing even faster than the rate of Moore's law. In supercomputing, the computational power increases by a factor of a thousand about every 10 years. Today's most powerful supercomputers are capable of performing around 10 exaFLOPS. (FLOPS is an acronym that stands for floating-point operations per second, and exa means 10^{18}.)

HPC can be exploited, for instance, in machine learning for training on very large data sets. Large AI question answering systems like IBM Watson would not be possible without using high-performance computing.

It is estimated that different kinds of computer devices, data centers, and computer networks in aggregate consume about 10% of the world's electricity. In addition, computer manufacturing also consumes a considerable amount of energy. This already makes the IT sector one of the major technological contributors to the global environmental impact of humankind. Moreover, the IT demand for power consumption is currently growing two times faster than the overall global power consumption. Today, humanity is facing serious environmental problems caused by climate change, which is in turn largely caused by uncontrolled power consumption. It may mean that in the near future IT power consumption should be reduced to mitigate the risks of climate change.

Using application-specific integrated circuits (ASICs) is one of the approaches for accelerating computing and making it more energy-efficient. An ASIC is a highly specialized version of an integrated circuit, best suited only to a very specific type of task. Application-specific integrated circuits massively outperform CPUs and even GPUs in computational efficiency at the task they have been designed for. Google's Tensor Processing Unit (TPU) is an example of ASIC specifically designed for neural network-based machine learning. Google has built huge supercomputers from multiple TPUs. It is believed that application-specific integrated circuits will be even more important for artificial intelligence in the future.

When it comes to simulating information processing that takes place in the human brain, it turns out that even the most advanced supercomputers are hideously inefficient in this process. These computers consume megawatts of electric power and are able to implement only a fraction of what the human brain does in terms of information processing, while the brain needs only 20 watts of energy.

An architecture of conventional computers, the von Neumann architecture, is based on the paradigm that memory and computational units are separate. The principles of the von Neumann architecture are different from the principles of information processing taking place in the biological brain. When we deal with the von Neumann architecture, we should constantly transfer information from computer memory to a CPU and backwards to enable computations. On the contrary, the structure of neuron connections itself represents memory in the brain.

It's widely accepted that the human brain is the most complex structure in the known universe. On average, the human brain has about 100 billion nerve cells (neurons) interlinked to each other by approximately 100 trillion - 1 billiard connections (synapses), comprising a gigantic neural network. It's interesting that there is a theory called the *integrated information theory*, which is shared by some well-known neuroscientists and physicists, including, for instance, Christof Koch and Max Tegmark. According to this theory, consciousness is a universal entity, and more complex structures can generate higher levels of consciousness, which explains why the brain is so complex. But this theory has several weak points.

Inspired by the human brain structure and functional capabilities, engineers started to develop a new, more efficient in many ways architecture of computational devices. This architecture is called neuromorphic computing. As the name suggests, neuromorphic computing imitates the functionality of the brain. There are different sub-types of this kind of architecture, but all of them share some common properties with each other. All neuromorphic circuits consist of multiple cores. Each of those cores is made of memory and computation units, so memory and computation are almost inseparable within these devices, but not completely. Also, there is an enlarged interconnection of the cores within these circuits. Some neuromorphic computing architectures use electronic analog circuits instead of digital ones. Also, there are other important distinctions.

In addition to just neuromorphic electronic architectures, there are even some hybrid neuro-computer architectures. For example, the project called Neu-ChiP led by a group of researchers at Aston University is aimed to directly combine human brain stem cells with silicon microchips.

Algorithms that can exploit the advantages of neuromorphic architectures are not sufficiently developed yet. This is especially relevant for artificial neural networks, which we will be discussing later.

Neuromorphic hardware is usually incredibly power efficient (by several orders of magnitude), compared to conventional computing. It's supposed that smartphones, tablets, and other portable devices will soon be based on neuromorphic hardware, and consequently, these devices will become much more computationally powerful.

In addition to bio-inspired computational devices, there are also neuromorphic sensory systems, for example, cameras imitating functions of the retina and microphones mimicking the neurobiological architecture of the human cochlea. Like neuromorphic computing hardware, such sensory approaches provide much lower power consumption compared to traditional ones.

However, some experts tend to suggest that neuromorphic computing is currently more some type of sophisticated hype stirring up by some companies seeking investors rather than a field actually capable of revolutionizing the computer industry.

At the end of this chapter, I should say that even if Moore's law continued for many decades, supercomputers occupied entire cities, and we were able to use tremendous unprecedented computational parallelism or advanced bio-inspired computing, many computational tasks would still remain intractable for us. Many such problems, however, could be efficiently solved on quantum computers.

Quantum Computing

There are certain limits of computation imposed by fundamental physical laws. The brilliant American scientist Seth Lloyd showed that 1 kg of matter can perform up to around 10^{50} operations per second. This staggering number is around 10^{36} times greater than what modern classical computers can squeeze out from 1 kg of matter per second. But it is believed that quantum computers can take us much closer to the ultimate limits of computation.

Quantum mechanics is an extremely counterintuitive theory and often considered very complicated. However, the renowned contemporary theorist in computational theory and quantum computing Scott Aaronson ironically says that quantum mechanics is an unbelievably simple concept once we take all the physics out of it. You can consider his book *Quantum computing since Democritus*.

Quantum mechanics describes systems which always stay at some level of uncertainty. Obviously, we use probability theory to deal with such systems. As we know from the theory of probability, the state of a system can be represented as a vector of nonnegative real numbers (probabilities of events) which have to add up to 1. However, in quantum mechanics instead of a vector of nonnegative real numbers, we have a vector of complex numbers, which are called amplitudes, and the sum of the squares of absolute values of these amplitudes has also to be equal to 1. The amplitudes can either be negative or positive, and it's important that these amplitudes can interfere with each other, which is called quantum interference. Whenever we measure a quantum system, these amplitudes (complex numbers) convert to square absolute values.

A quantum computer exploits quantum interference. In fact, the main advantage of quantum computing over classical computing is the quantum interference of the amplitudes which can cancel each other out. In quantum computers, we arrange our computations in such a way, where the paths to wrong answers have negative and positive amplitudes canceling each other out, whereas the paths leading to correct answers have amplitudes of the same sign.

Quantum computers operate qubits or quantum bits which have to stay in quantum coherence with each other during computations. A qubit is a 2-level quantum system, which means that this system can be in two distinguishable states. During computation, qubits are in both these states simultaneously, which calls superposition, and quantum interference can occur when qubits are in the state of superposition. Once we measure the system, the state of superposition disappears.

A quantum computer with n qubits can be in 2^n states. Probably, the most remarkable feature of these machines is that the computational power of a quantum computer doubles with each additional qubit for some computational tasks. That is, a quantum computer with 300 qubits is 2^{100} times more computationally powerful for such tasks than a quantum computer with 200 qubits. We should say that classical computers with n bits can be in 2^n distinguishable states too, but classical bits cannot exploit quantum superposition, so such a speedup of computations does not occur in classical computers.

A qubit can be any 2-level quantum system, for example, a photon polarized horizontally or vertically, an electron with two spinning states, or an ion at a ground or excited level. Due to this diversity, there are different types of possible architectures for quantum computers.

The outcome, one receives from a quantum computer is always probabilistic. This means that in order to obtain reliable results from a quantum computer, it is often necessary to run the quantum algorithm many times on the same data and choose the outcome that occurs most frequently.

Like conventional computers, quantum computers have basic operating units, in this case, called quantum logic gates. The process of computation on quantum computers is applying these logic gates to qubits and measuring the state of the qubits at the end of the computation. Quantum computers are able to perform all operations performed by classical computers, and some of the operations can be performed much more efficiently on quantum computers.

The class of computational problems which can be efficiently (in polynomial time) solved by quantum computing is called BQP. This class extends the class P, so quantum computers can efficiently solve more problems than classical computers can. However, we do not have any evidence that quantum computers can solve NP-complete problems in polynomial time.

In addition to reducing the number of computational steps, some quantum algorithms can supply one other important advantage to speed up computations. This advantage is reducing the number of accesses to the computer memory. But this memory has to be quantum too, which means that classical data should be encoded as a set of quantum states. Building such a quantum random access memory is a currently unsolved engineering problem.

Probably, the most preeminent application for quantum computers is the simulation of quantum systems. In fact, quantum computers were proposed for this task in the early 1980s. Classical computers cannot simulate quantum systems efficiently. Scientists have long been inventing different heuristic techniques which can basically give only approximate outcomes, and yet requiring gigantic supercomputers, which consume tremendous amounts of energy for simulating relatively small quantum systems like middle-sized molecules. On the other hand, universal quantum computers would be an ideal computational environment for such tasks. Using a relatively small quantum computer, consisting of several hundreds of qubits would allow achieving the results in modeling and designing quantum systems, which cannot be achieved using only classical computers. Calculations which are possible with quantum computers can blur the line between different natural disciplines, such as physics, chemistry, and even biology, which we use in the study of the world today.

For pure classical applications, there is also a great practical interest in devising quantum algorithms that have a computational advantage over the best classical algorithms known for the same tasks. The first and probably most famous quantum algorithm is Shor's algorithm for factoring numbers, which was proposed by Peter Shor in 1994. This algorithm has an exponential speedup over its classical counterpart. It is noteworthy that the implementation of this algorithm on very powerful quantum computers would enable breaking almost all current encryption systems, and this is likely the major reason why in the 1990s many countries launched their programs to develop quantum computers.

Another famous quantum algorithm is Grover's algorithm for search over unstructured data, which was devised by the Indian-American computer scientist Lov Grover in 1996. This algorithm has a quadratic speedup over its equivalent classical counterpart; a quadratic speedup is not exponential, but even such a speedup is often considerable. For example, if an original 2^n algorithm requires 2^{10} steps, an algorithm with a quadratic speedup would require 2^5 steps. The search over unstructured data occurs in a very broad category of computational problems, including many tasks of artificial intelligence.

Quantum algorithms can be used in machine learning. Machine learning is an indispensable part of modern artificial intelligence. Seth Lloyd says that the main principle of the majority of machine learning algorithms is linear algebra on high-dimensional vector spaces, and quantum mechanics is also all about linear algebra on high-dimensional vector spaces, so it's very likely that quantum computing can effectively solve many machine learning tasks.

In 2009, Aram Harrow, Avinatan Hassidim, and Seth Lloyd formulated a quantum algorithm for solving linear systems of equations (HHL algorithm). Like Shor's algorithm, the HHL algorithm provides an exponential speedup over its best classical counterparts. It can also be applied to a broad area of computational tasks, many of which belong to machine learning.

In addition, there are many proposals of hybrid approaches, where quantum computers can be used in conjunction with classical computers for solving some computational tasks.

The most important problem in building quantum computers is the decoherence of the qubits. In 1995, it was shown that this problem can be successfully mitigated by the set of techniques called quantum error correction. Quantum error correction allows building machines where not all the qubits have to be in perfect quantum coherence with each other during computation. It was a very important breakthrough at that time, and since then it has become clear that building reliable quantum computers is not a scientific but a pure engineering problem. Quantum error correction exploits the redundancy of the qubits inside quantum chips.

Building big, powerful quantum computers with many reliable qubits is still an unsolved engineering problem, but quantum computers are gradually becoming more powerful.

When practical quantum computers are built, they will probably be in the cloud for commercial use. In fact, IBM claims that they already provide free access to a 5-qubit quantum computer via the IBM cloud, on which it is possible to play around with quantum algorithms.

The Canadian company *D-Wave Systems* claims that they have manufactured the first commercially available quantum computers. Recently, D-Wave has released its new computer named *2000Q* after the number of qubits within its chip.

However, it's widely accepted, that D-Wave's machines are not universal quantum computers. Each qubit within D-Wave's chips is only connected to at most six other qubits. The time for which the qubits inside D-Wave's chips can stay in superposition is extremely short, so it is not possible to apply quantum logic gates to these qubits. These machines are capable of solving combinatorial optimization problems. (We will be discussing optimization problems in one of the following chapters.) D-Wave's computers use so-called quantum adiabatic algorithms, and we still don't know whether these algorithms can give any computational speedup over the best classical algorithms for the same problems.

Many respected experts from academia, including the above-mentioned scientist Scott Aaronson, have skeptically criticized claims that these machines can provide any supremacy over classical computers. Rather, according to these experts, D-Wave's computers are special-purpose classical computational devices, which do use some quantum effects, but these effects don't provide any computational speedup.

Despite considerable criticism, D-Wave's computers can be considered true technological marvels, and plenty of researchers and engineers are paying close attention to these machines. Moreover, several companies, including Google and Lockheed Martin, have bought a few D-Wave's computers. Reportedly, Google, for example, tests the computational capabilities of these devices for machine learning applications.

At the end of this chapter, I should say that there is a hypothesis that the biological brain can perform some quantum algorithms. This hypothesis was even discussed in authoritative scientific journals. However, it was criticized and virtually dismissed by the mainstream scientific community. Although it's not entirely clear how the brain process information and how consciousness arises, it's thought that the brain is a classical information processing system, and there is no need for quantum effects to describe such a system. In particular, neural networks in the brain are classical systems which process information. But it's always a good idea to stay open-minded.

Artificial Intelligence and Machine Learning

Like the term "intelligence", the term "artificial intelligence" has many definitions as well. According to most of them, a key feature of artificial intelligence is the ability to mimic humans. The definition that I came across at the online computer dictionary http://techterms.com/ says: "Artificial Intelligence, or AI, is the ability of a computer to act like a human being." Definitions of AI we can find in other sources are similar to that.

It's curious that when a certain program starts to perform functions that have been traditionally considered as a prerogative of humans, these functions stop being regarded as a human prerogative anymore. For example, in the 50s and 60s of the 20th century, computers were often called *thinking machines*, and they really could be called so, because they performed the work – different mathematical calculations – that had been carried out by people before them, and it is remarkable that those people were also called computers. But soon afterward such mathematical capabilities were regarded as totally trivial for computers.

In addition to mimicking humans, we can also think of artificial intelligence, as a set of clever techniques for obtaining reasonably appropriate solutions to hard NP problems.

In practical terms, there have been distinguished two main classes of AI: narrow AI and general AI. A narrow AI system can perform only very specific types of actions. On the contrary, general AI is a system that can perform a wide variety of different tasks.

Narrow artificial intelligence is almost everywhere in the computer world today. It is used, for example, in speech and image recognition, weather forecasting, self-driving cars, page ranking by search engines, product recommendations by e-stores, or friend recommendations by social media. We could continue this list with a tremendous number of other various applications of narrow AI.

On the other hand, we don't have artificial general intelligence – a kind of intelligence that can successfully perform any intellectual tasks that a human being can, and even more than that.

Artificial intelligence is now a very broad scientific and engineering subject with many various algorithms and computational approaches.

Traditional approaches in AI – sometimes called Good Old Fashion AI (GOFAI) – are mostly based on operating with symbolic logic. In this approach, concepts and statements are represented as symbols. These symbols can then be manipulated based on the rules of logic to produce new statements. In such systems, a component that applies logical rules to the symbols is called the *inference engine*. Often, GOFAI approaches use many clever heuristics.

Many problems in AI can be thought of as search problems. For example, an AI system can search for the best solution to some problem. Search algorithms have been widely applied in AI game-playing systems and some other tasks. There are many kinds of search algorithms in symbolic AI. Search can be implemented either when we exactly know the state of the world (deterministic search) or under some level of uncertainty (non-deterministic search). Not surprisingly, the later version of the search is more suitable for solving real-world problems than the first one.

There is an important method for decision making under uncertainty, which is applied in a variety of applications, for example in robotics. This method is called Markov decision process (MDP) (named after the famous Russian mathematician Andrey Markov). MDP provides a general framework for non-deterministic search algorithms. Markov decision process is a sequential process of planning under uncertainty. In this method, the plan of actions to take is called policy. MDP is applied not only in symbolic AI. MDP is at the core of reinforcement machine learning.

In principle, some tasks of symbolic AI can be more efficiently performed by using quantum computing. As we have seen in the previous chapter, there is a quantum algorithm that implements search in unstructured data better than any classical algorithms do. There are some proposals for using quantum algorithms for building symbolic rules-based AI systems. For example, there is the *quantum tree search algorithm* and *quantum production system.* (In artificial intelligence, a production system is basically a set of rules to manipulate knowledge.)

Another example of symbolic AI systems is expert systems. These systems can be viewed as the storages of human knowledge, which is represented in a symbolic form, in specific domains combined with handcrafted logic rules that describe how to manipulate this knowledge. The knowledge is often collected by interviewing a large number of experts in a particular domain. Of course, this is a prominent impediment to building such systems. Expert systems do work in their domains, but they cannot learn from experience and require being painstakingly preprogrammed and even completely reprogrammed for other tasks.

The symbolic approach in AI is still in use. For example, expert systems are still being used in some domains. Even IBM's Watson system can be viewed as a very large expert system which has machine learning components.

There have been even attempts – for instance, the Cyc project – to create artificial general intelligence by building a huge symbolic expert system in which all human knowledge and rules about how the world works would be incorporated, but these attempts have failed so far.

Even though symbolic approaches in AI can produce some valuable results, these techniques have fallen into disfavor mainly because of two factors: first, their inability to adapt to a complex, ever-changing environment, and their requirement of being painstakingly preprogrammed with a huge amount of handcrafted rules. There is also one more important factor: combinatorial explosion. In an expert system, the number of possible inferences grows exponentially with the growth of the knowledge base of this system.

It is widely accepted today that artificial general intelligence cannot be created by using only symbolic logic-based strategies. Due to the complexity of the world, it's very difficult to write such programs, especially from scratch, for a constantly changing environment.

This also holds true for pattern recognition. For example, if we wanted to write a computer program to tell the difference between images of apples and oranges, we could come up with an astonishingly complex program. But if we changed some parameters of the images like size or color, our super complex program would most likely not work appropriately anymore, and we would again need to write a new program.

Instead, the approaches in AI incorporated with some form of learning – like the examples of narrow AI mentioned above – have gained many practically valuable achievements.

Machine learning algorithms can learn from and make predictions on data. Machine learning gives computer programs a remarkable ability to adapt to changes in an environment and learn from experience. This is the most important feature of machine learning.

Machine learning, statistics, and the theory of optimization are closely related fields. A machine learning approach is all about building statistical models. I will not go into the math here, but only mention a few concepts at a very abstract level. Machine learning can be viewed as a form of applied statistics for solving various optimization problems. In short, mathematical optimization is a process of minimization or maximization of a certain function, most often minimization (but it doesn't really matter).

In mathematics, a function is a certain rule that assigns to each element of the first set one and only one element from the second set. It can be also viewed as a certain type of relation. Any process in the world can be thought of as a function.

Sometimes, the optimization of a function is a straightforward task. However, most optimization problems are NP-hard problems.

In principle, we could try to solve optimization problems just by applying brute-force search through the variables, but it wouldn't be a very clever strategy, of course. There are various cleverer methods for solving optimization problems. In machine learning, most such methods belong to so-called gradient-based optimization. The most common method applied in machine learning is called stochastic gradient descent. Although gradient-based optimization methods are quite effective, they have some disadvantages.

Interestingly, it has been assumed that quantum annealing can perform optimization tasks faster than classical gradient-based optimization methods, but it has not been proved. Furthermore, Grover's quantum algorithm in principle can be used instead of gradient-based optimization in some machine learning programs such as artificial neural networks.

Nowadays, artificial intelligence has greatly shifted towards utilizing machine learning approaches. Even the term "Machine learning" is now more popular and frequently used than "Artificial intelligence".

In general, different machine learning algorithms fall into three broad categories: supervised, unsupervised, and reinforcement machine learning approaches.

Supervised learning is a type of learning where pieces of training data are labeled with descriptions or values. Based on such training labeled data, supervised learning algorithms can generate values of unlabeled data. For example, we can "show" millions of labeled images of cars to a supervised machine learning program, and after this training, the program will be able to recognize cars in unlabeled images.

Supervised learning itself consists of two subcategories: regression and classification. Regression is such a sub-type of supervised learning when input data are labeled with real numbers; whereas classification is a sub-type where labels represent classes. Currently, supervised machine learning gives the most practical results in comparison to other types of ML, but it also has a serious disadvantage: data labeling is a tedious task and often requires a lot of work which has to be done by humans.

In the case of unsupervised learning, however, we don't have labeled training data, and the algorithms have to extract hidden patterns in unlabeled data. Broadly speaking, the aim of unsupervised learning is discovering meaningful patterns in data sets. A typical task of unsupervised learning is clustering. Clustering is a process of finding groups of similar objects in a dataset. Although this task can seem trivial at a first glance, in reality, it can be quite complicated. It turns out that there are numerous methods to measure similarity or distance between data points, and there is no consensus on which method works best.

There is a practical interest in using unsupervised learning: the majority of data on the Internet as well as in other sources is unlabeled. Also, unsupervised learning can be used in order to create an internal representation of the data, and this representation can increase the efficiency of subsequent supervised or reinforcement learning algorithms.

Despite important achievements in recent years, so far unsupervised learning hasn't been as successful as supervised machine learning. In the opinion of Yann LeCun, Director of AI Research at Facebook, unsupervised learning is a key component for acquiring common sense by computational machines. Also, he believes that adopting powerful unsupervised learning algorithms will allow building predictive AI systems, similar to natural intelligence because natural intelligence is largely based on the unsupervised type of learning. Further development of powerful unsupervised machine learning algorithms is one of the crucial components for creating strong artificial general intelligence.

The third type of machine learning is reinforcement learning. Reinforcement learning is a sequential decision process. The interaction of a machine learning system with a real or virtual world lies at the heart of reinforcement learning. In reinforcement learning, an ML agent or system has a goal or a set of goals. The ML agent observes its environment and has to decide what actions to take to achieve its goals. The agent gets a numerical reward whenever it chooses the actions that lead to achieving its goals. So, the agent becomes better at achieving goals as it iterates many cycles of training. This model is very similar to biology. In our brain, we have a similar mechanism: it's called a dopamine reward system.

Recently, the usage of reinforcement learning has yielded some very encouraging results, for example, computer game-playing systems which are able to quickly learn how to play a variety of computer games without being pre-programmed. The reward, in this case, is winning the game or getting maximum scores. These game-playing systems implement general-purpose (to some extent) learning algorithms. Such algorithms learn automatically from raw inputs and do not require being pre-programmed for new similar tasks. Demis Hassabis, a co-founder and CEO of the artificial intelligence company *DeepMind*, says that these systems can be viewed as a microcosm of artificial general intelligence. It is assumed that similar approaches will be widely adopted in robotics, where robots will learn from scratch and work with real physical objects.

However, there are a couple of concerns towards using reinforcement learning in physical world applications like robotics. First, if we use only reinforcement learning, in many physical environments, the agent can make fatal mistakes very quickly, resulting in breaking the agent or other accidents or unrecoverable errors. Second, even if the agent managed not to make such mistakes, the learning process would be prohibitively slow: we can't run the world quicker than it does on its own. Instead, we should simulate the world or in other words predict the future state of the world and put the agent in this model. So, here comes the necessity of unsupervised learning.

Combining all the three types of machine learning into a single program which is capable of performing different tasks is currently an important challenge for ML.

In every machine learning project, there are two main stages: training and inferencing (making predictions). Actually, there also other stages – like data preparation, testing, and validation – but for simplicity, we can omit them in this discussion. During training, we supply a machine learning algorithm with training data. In this process, the algorithm produces a model. And then, we can use this model for making predictions.

In one of the first chapters, we saw that algorithms may be relatively computationally simple or may require enormous amounts of computational resources. But another important characteristic of an algorithm is its capacity for people to understand it. For example, an algorithm can be relatively computationally simple, but at the same time it may require, say, a thousand lines of code in a high-level programming language or, say, a million machine instructions. Such an algorithm would be tremendously difficult to understand and tune, let alone create one. We can view machine learning algorithms as the algorithms that produce new algorithms during training. Of course, those produced algorithms are never written in any high-level programming language; they are nothing more than generated sequences of machine instructions. Those sequences of machine instructions are usually very complex, and without machine learning, it would be enormously difficult and maybe even practically impossible to produce them.

There are a variety of traditional small machine learning algorithms. One important disadvantage of many traditional ML algorithms is that people have to carefully and thoughtfully prepare data for them. This data preparation usually includes such processes called feature extraction and feature selection. But it is very difficult to do manually for such complex types of data as images or audio records. Because of this, most ML algorithms are not suitable for solving such complex problems like image and speech recognition. By the way, the interpretation of the results of many ML algorithms also often requires thoughtful analysis, especially for unsupervised ones.

One particular subfield of machine learning has become an especially promising area of research and practical applications in the last decade. This subfield is enticingly called *deep learning*, which is a suitable tool for more complex tasks and which we will be discussing in the next chapter.

Artificial Neural Networks and Deep Learning

Like artificial intelligence, machine learning is a very broad area with plenty of various computational techniques, but, currently, one particular branch of ML is becoming more widespread in comparison to the others for solving complex problems. This is artificial neural networks. Currently, deep neural networks usually outperform other machine learning techniques in the field of artificial intelligence. However, despite recent tangible progress in neural networks, many other branches of ML are also extremely important and interesting.

This chapter is by no means a complete overview of artificial neural networks, but rather only a brief, math-free introduction into the field, which is constantly growing. Artificial neural networks are the hottest area of research in artificial intelligence right now, and numerous publications on neural networks appear around the world every day.

Now, artificial neural networks (ANNs) or just neural nets are basically certain types of software for classical computers. Neural nets have been known in the computer industry since the late 1950s, but they have shown great results in practical applications and gained extraordinary popularity only relatively recently.

The recent successes of neural networks can be explained by three major factors. First, in the beginning, ANNs were very simple (actually they were pieces of special analog hardware, known as perceptrons), and could perform only relatively simple types of tasks. So, many more complex computational problems became tractable by neural networks only after new, more elaborate algorithms and empirical tricks – like some training methods, for example – had been developed for artificial neural networks. Second, computational resources have become powerful enough to run those advanced neural networks also only relatively recently. In particular, using GPUs has given a speedup of a factor of 50 and even more for neural networks and other machine learning algorithms. And the third factor is the abundance of data in a digital format necessary to train ANNs that have become available with the spread of the internet and cyberspace. For instance, due to the project ImageNet, millions of labeled images became available in the 2000s. Usually, training deep neural networks requires larger amounts of data than training traditional machine learning algorithms.

At a super abstract level, artificial neural nets' work somewhat resembles the activity of biological neural networks in the brain. Like biological neural networks, ANNs consist of a large number of computational units (neurons or nodes) which are interconnected with each other. However, the relationship between artificial neural networks and biological neural networks is still mostly metaphorical and inspirational. By the way, some experts believe that the tendency of thinking of artificial neural networks from a neuroscience perspective is actually detrimental due to the fact that artificial neural networks don't really work as their biological counterparts. Rather, it would be probably more appropriate to think of ANNs from pure mathematics or computer science perspective.

Generally, in each artificial neural network, there is an input layer, an output layer, and one or more hidden layers of neurons. The input layer performs no computations and only receives information in a digital format. Then, this information is processed mostly in the hidden layers. The output layer of neurons gives new information, which represents a solution to some computational problem.

Artificial neural networks with several hidden layers have an important advantage over shallow ones. Multi-layered neural nets can effectively process data in more complex patterns and to some extent automate the process of feature engineering, which is the main obstacle for traditional machine learning algorithms. Multi-layered networks are able to break down complex patterns into simpler components. Such multi-layered neural nets are called *deep neural networks* (DNNs).

According to the *universal approximation theorem*, a neural network that has only one hidden layer can approximate any continuous function, but the hidden layer must grow exponentially with the size of the input. Because of this, neural networks with more than one hidden layer are used for solving complex tasks with large inputs. Technically, any neural network with more than one hidden layer is deep, but, in most situations, neural networks are called "deep" only if they have at least a dozen of hidden layers.

Advancement in deep neural networks has spawned the practical field of *deep learning*. Deep learning has captivated the headlines in recent years. Formally speaking, deep learning is a process of building functions from many smaller nested functions and then performing optimization on them. It can be implemented in many ways, but the most common approach is carried out by utilizing artificial neural networks. In contrast to traditional machine learning algorithms, the main idea of deep learning is building machine learning models that consist of multiple layers of abstractions, where the higher layers use the outputs of the lower layers.

As we said, feature extraction is one of the weakest points of traditional machine learning algorithms. There is so-called *representation learning* or *feature learning*, where a machine learning algorithm tries to find an appropriate representation of data for implementing the consequent task. Deep learning exploits this process by its very nature. So far, representation learning has been the main advantage of deep learning over traditional machine learning approaches. Representation learning can be both supervised and unsupervised.

The field of deep learning has a long and rich history. I will mention here only its several pivotal points. The concept of deep learning was introduced by two Ukrainian mathematicians Alexey Ivakhnenko, who is sometimes referred to as the "father of deep learning", and Valentine Lapa in the distant 1965. The phrase "deep learning" was coined by Rina Dechter in 1986. In 1989, Yann LeCun successfully applied the back-propagation algorithm to deep neural networks to recognize handwritten ZIP codes on pieces of mail. In 1997, long short term memory (LSTM) networks were invented by Sepp Hochreiter and Jürgen Schmidhuber. In 2009, it was shown that deep neural networks could be successfully used for speech recognition. In 2012, Geoffrey Hinton stunned the world when he with his team won an important image recognition competition by using deep neural networks. Since then, a plethora of other impressive achievements have been accomplished by using deep neural networks.

It is extremely important that we can build any possible logic gates by connecting neurons in neural networks in a specific fashion. This means that neural networks are computationally universal. In mathematical parlance, a neural network is a universal function approximator that can approximate any function.

Like other machine learning algorithms, artificial neural networks can produce algorithmic solutions to many computational problems that haven't had *known* algorithmic solutions before.

Similar to other machine learning approaches, the work of artificial neural networks consists of two main phases: training and inferencing. For most types of ANNs, the training phase is much more computationally intensive than a single inference. However, a trained neural network is used for making thousands or even millions of inferences, usually making the inference stage more computationally intensive than the training phase.

In one of the first chapters, we saw that the IT industry has become one of the main components of global energy consumption and thus carbon emission. And it absolutely applies to the field of deep learning. In fact, training modern state-of-the-art deep neural networks requires tremendous amounts of energy. For example, in 2020 OpenAI trained a gigantic deep neural network, named GPT-3, that had 175 billion learnable parameters. It is estimated that generating the amount of energy needed for training such a giant neural network releases 5-50 million kilograms of CO_2 if the energy were produced from fuel combustion. As a point of comparison, an average car emits around 5 thousand kilograms of CO_2 in a year. Moreover, the overall inference stage requires even more energy. Thus, the negative environmental impact in terms of power consumption and carbon emission may soon become a serious impediment to using deep learning on a massive scale unless more efficient algorithms and hardware become available.

The basic idea behind ANNs is very simple: it's an error correction model. Each artificial neuron is a computational unit that can adjust its parameters – which are called weights – based on the inputs from other units it's connected to. Neurons adjust their parameters after comparing neural network's outputs with correct answers during training cycles. The weights (as well as some other parameters) in neural networks are also called free parameters.

Actually, the training of artificial neural networks is a hard computational problem. For training neural networks, some algorithms have been developed, which give approximate results for finding the values of neural networks' free parameters. The most popular algorithm is called the back-propagation algorithm, often called backprop.

Actually, there are two main training algorithms in an artificial neural network; back-propagation does only part of the job. The other algorithm is almost always based on gradient optimization, and most often it is stochastic gradient descent or some version of it.

Most practical achievements in deep artificial neural networks have been accomplished by using backprop. The back-propagation algorithm is quite simple, but the mathematical details of it lie beyond the scope of this entirely conceptual book. If you know calculus, you can easily understand how this algorithm works. By the way, you don't even have to know all calculus to understand this algorithm. Back-propagation is an applied form of the chain rule with memorization of previously computed values.

Despite the great achievements, the back-propagation algorithm and gradient-based optimization have considerable computational drawbacks.

Gradient-based optimization is an iterative process of finding the global minimum of a function by calculating the gradients and applying gradual movement towards the minimum. But gradient descent has a quite serious disadvantage because the iterative process of gradient descent can get stuck in one of the local minima instead of finding the global minima of the function. This problem had been one of the major drawbacks to using neural networks for a long time. However, it turns out that, in networks that have numerous learnable parameters, the gradient descent algorithm indeed almost always gets stuck in one of the function's local minima, but this local minimum is very close to the global minimum. The local minima problem is not so serious anymore, but it is always there anyway.

Also, there is a problem called *vanishing gradient*, and it is usually more difficult than the local minima problem. The vanishing gradient problem occurs in neural networks with many hidden layers.

In addition to that, there are other even more important limitations and disadvantages of this algorithm for building really intelligent machines that can learn in an unsupervised way. The brilliant British cognitive psychologist and computer scientist Geoffrey Hinton, one of the leading researchers in deep learning, says that he does not think that the back-propagation algorithm is the path to building artificial general intelligence.

In terms of high topology, there are two main types of artificial neural networks: feed-forward, and recurrent ANNs. There are also symmetrically connected neural networks and many subtypes.

Different types of neural nets are not equally suited for different computational tasks.

In feed-forward ANNs, information flows only in one direction – from input to output. Feed-forward neural nets are currently used in most pattern recognition applications.

In a neural network, layers of neurons can be either fully-connected, where each neuron is connected to all neurons from the previous layer, or partially connected.

Convolutional neural networks (CNNs or ConvNets) are a subcategory of feed-forward nets with partially connected layers. For tasks in which repetitive spacial patterns can be found – for example, it can be an image with some repetitive edges and other patterns – CNNs are more computationally efficient than fully-connected feed-forward nets allowing for using computational resources much more efficiently. Currently, the process of image recognition is implemented primarily by applying CNNs. These networks are also employed for a wide variety of other tasks. Currently, convolutional neural networks are the most frequently used type of ANNs.

Convolutional networks usually have several hidden layers. Hidden layers that are closer to the input layer detect very simple features like edges and color gradients in the images. Then, the higher layers combine those simple features in more complex patterns. Finally, the layers that are close to the output combine those patterns. Interestingly, the structure of convolutional neural networks was initially inspired by studying the organization of the animal visual cortex. Employing CNNs for image recognition in the early 1990s was the first practical success of artificial neural networks. CNNs have already achieved superhuman performance at some image recognition tasks. However, these networks have also some serious drawbacks.

There are also so-called *capsule neural networks*. Recently Geoffrey Hinton with co-authors published a paper on these networks: https://arxiv.org/abs/1710.09829. In this paper, they introduced an algorithm to train such networks, called *dynamic routing between capsules*. Most ANNs have two levels of structure: a neuron and a layer of neurons. The main idea behind capsule neural networks that differentiates them from other types of ANNs is that capsule neural networks have a new level of structure. This level is formed by incorporating a special entity, called a *capsule*. A capsule is inspired by a mini-column in the neocortex of the brain. It is more biology-realistic than two-dimensional ANNs. In fact, the brain is a three-dimensional neural network.

Capsule neural networks can be viewed as a potential replacement for convolutional networks for visual pattern recognition and probably some other tasks. It has been shown that capsule networks outperform convolutional networks by a significant margin in tasks where images are taken from different perspectives or partially occluded.

Another broad category of ANNs is *recurrent networks*. Generally speaking, recurrent neural networks are a more elaborate type of ANNs than feed-forward nets. A feed-forward network can only process inputs of the same size. For processing variable-size inputs, recurrent networks are used. Recurrent networks are much more powerful in what they can do but also much more difficult to train in comparison to feed-forward ANNs. Recurrent nets can receive a sequence of inputs and generate a sequence of outputs. Neurons in their hidden layers have recurrent connections. These networks can predict the next item in a sequence, so they can be used for forecasting. It's important that recurrent networks are more biologically realistic than feed-forward nets: the cortex in the brain is a fully recurrent neural network.

A recursive neural network is a subtype of recurrent networks. A typical recursive neural network has a tree-like structure. Recursive as well as other types of recurrent networks have been employed, for instance, in natural language processing (NLP).

Language is one of the key manifestations of human intelligence. It is even believed that we will have AGI when machines master natural language. Recent advances in NLP are amazing, although there is still an almost unlimited amount of work to do for computer scientists in this domain. Now machines can understand spoken and written language and in many cases produce meaningful to us sentences. Usually, building natural language processing systems based on deep learning does not require any linguists at all, as opposed to old school symbolic NLP, which was based on numerous human-crafted linguistic rules. There are many digital assistants such as Siri, Google Assistance, Cortana, Alexa, incorporated with NLP based on deep learning.

I should say here that the output – as well as the input – of any artificial neural network is a vector. A vector is basically a string of numbers. For example, [0.51 0.23 0.88 0.12 0.94] is a vector consisted of 5 numbers, or we can say that the dimensionality of this vector is 5. The dimensionality of the outputs of some deep neural networks can be large.

In deep learning based NLP, we can represent words as vectors consisting of different values of real numbers (it is called *distributed word representation*), and we can do arithmetic and algebraic operations with such vectors. For example, we can subtract one vector from another vector of the same dimensionality. We can also compare such vectors with each other.

Instead in classical rule-based NLP, words were regarded as atomic structures. We can represent this representation as vectors of zeros with only a one single one value, for example, like [0 0 0 1 0 0]. This is called a one-hot encoding. There are many problems with this approach. First, we have to work with vectors of humongous dimensionality. For instance, if we are working with a language consisting, say, of 150000 words, the dimensionality of our vectors is 150000. The second and even bigger problem is that we can't really measure the similarity between such vectors. Because of this, we can't establish relations between such vectors.

By adopting the new, neural network-based approach to NLP search engines, for instance, work much better. They can understand, for example, that such words as car, auto, or automobile represent basically the same concept. So, when we type in a search box one of these words, the search engine may suggest web pages, where this exact word does not appear at all.

We can make computers manipulate distributed word vectors. A canonical example of such manipulations is

WOMAN – MAN + QUEEN = KING

It means that if we subtract the vector "man" from the vector "woman" and add the vector "queen", we get the vector that is very close to the vector "king". This is a very trivial example, of course, but, by doing such operations with word vectors, in principle, we can obtain new knowledge. Not only can we do such manipulations with individual words but also with entire sentences and even larger text fragments. Recursive neural networks were specifically designed for building vector representations for text fragments from vector representations of individual words.

Currently in NLP, a distributed word representation vector for some word is built by analyzing the context that appears around this word. This approach is called word embedding. Words that appear in similar contexts have similar distributed word representations.

However, there are certain limitations in adopting this approach. First and foremost, although words with similar vectors are closely related to each other, having very similar distributed word representations of words does not actually mean that these words are synonyms to each other. For example, the closest vector to the vector of the word "synonym" corresponds to the word "antonym" in the framework of word embedding.

Some state-of-the-art architectures of deep neural networks combine both computer vision and natural language processing. This architecture allows the machines to find correlations between language and visual information. For example, such systems can automatically produce quite accurate descriptions of images. Or conversely, they can produce images when they are given descriptions.

Although systems with NLP based on deep learning can give meaningful sentences and correct answers to some simple questions, they are not really capable of what we refer to as thinking or reasoning, largely because they don't have their models of the world. I will return to discussing this in the next chapter.

Recurrent neural networks can remember their previous states, but not for very long. Most recurrent nets forget their initial states after about twenty iterations. If they remembered, they would become prohibitively difficult to train. It's interesting that this is somewhat similar to the processing taking place in the brain. The problem with learning long-term dependencies in recurrent networks occurs due to the vanishing gradient problem, which we've previously mentioned in this chapter. A recurrent neural network with just a single hidden layer can actually be viewed as a neural network with many hidden layers because the neurons in the hidden layer not only have connections with the input layer but also with the neurons of the same layer.

A long *short-term memory (LSTM) network* is a subtype of recurrent neural networks. LSTM networks have special memory cells which allow these nets to remember their state for longer periods of time. Such architecture has a very important advantage over a vanilla RNN in terms of the susceptibility to the vanishing gradient problem. Therefore, LSTM networks learn long-term dependencies much better than simple RNNs. LSTM networks have been successfully employed in many applications, such as natural language processing, speech recognition, handwriting generation, machine translation, and image captioning.

In addition to LSTMs, there are other types of neural networks augmented with a memory like, for example, a Neural Turing Machine, Differentiable Neural Computer, and Stack Augmented Recurrent Neural Network. Recently, a new strategy for augmenting ANNs with memory has been proposed, which is called the Recurrent Entity Network (EntNet) (https://arxiv.org/pdf/1612.03969.pdf).

Also, different types of neural networks can be combined in a more complex neural network. For example, there are so-called convolutional recurrent neural networks (CRNNs). In other approaches, different types of neural networks, though not combined, work in collaboration with each other. For example, in some applications, the output of a recurrent neural network can be fed into a convolutional network.

So far, we have been mostly discussing neural networks for supervised learning tasks. As we said, most practical results in deep learning have been achieved in supervised learning. However, neural networks can be used for unsupervised learning as well. There are certain types of artificial neural networks specifically designed for this type of learning.

An *autoencoder* is a typical artificial neural network being used for unsupervised learning. An autoencoder consists of two main parts: encoder and decoder. Also, an autoencoder has a middle layer, which is responsible for the lower-dimensional representation of the data. The encoder encodes the input in a lower dimension, then the decoder reconstructs the input again. At first sight, this process may seem absolutely useless, but actually, autoencoders can be very useful. First of all, an autoencoder is a data compression technique. Also, autoencoders can be used to facilitate the work of supervised learning, such as classification tasks, when we don't have a significant amount of labeled data. In addition, autoencoders can be used for generative modeling and some other tasks.

Self-organizing maps (SOMs) are a very interesting type of ANNs for unsupervised learning. SOMs were invented by the Finnish professor Teuvo Kohonen, so they are also known as Kohonen nets. They have been known since the 1980s. These networks have only two layers, so they don't belong to deep learning, and they don't have much in common with other types of artificial neural networks. These networks can convert multi-dimensional data into data of smaller dimensionality, and then this new representation of the data can be employed for visualization or clustering, for instance. These networks have been successfully used in many domains.

A *Hopfield network* is another type of neural network for unsupervised learning. Hopfield networks do not use the backpropagation algorithm, and they are not deep. These networks store associative memories, which then can be retrieved. Interestingly, it is somewhat similar to the brain because memories in the brain are associative.

In addition, there are other very interesting neural network-based approaches for unsupervised learning. However, as we have said earlier, unsupervised deep learning is still rather underdeveloped. Developing new forms of effective deep unsupervised learning is an imperative task for building artificial general intelligence.

Applications with deep learning have gained many impressive results for solving real-world problems in many domains. Deep networks can effectively do both perception and generation of new patterns. The problem of perception has been recently mostly solved by deep learning. About 10-15 years ago computers could not compete with humans in object recognition, and people believed that perception was the trait completely belonging to the realm of biological intelligence. But modern deep neural nets can recognize some types of patterns even better than humans can. However, there is still a great deal of work in this domain of deep learning.

The field of pattern generation by deep neural networks is also tremendously growing. This is known as generative modeling. Generative models produce new samples given training data without using any labels; therefore they belong to unsupervised learning. For example, given a set of images, a generative model can generate similar, convincingly looking images. It is assumed that a large portion of the content on the web may be produced by generative models in the near future. Generative models can be used for simulation, planning, and even some form of reasoning.

The main idea of generative modeling can be explained as follows: first, a machine learning algorithm such as a neural network learns the underlying function that describes the distribution of the training data, and then the algorithm generates brand new samples of the same distribution. There are different ANN architectures that can be used for generative modeling.

One of the popular neural network architectures for generative modeling is a *variational autoencoder*. This is a special type of autoencoder in which the latent representation layer is slightly modified than in a traditional autoencoder. After training, a variational autoencoder can generate new data by tuning the values of its latent variables.

An interesting subtype of a variational autoencoder is a so-called *disentangled variational autoencoder*. This subtype of an autoencoder has uncorrelated variables in its latent representation.

In 2014, Ian Goodfellow proposed a new and very interesting type of neural networks called *Generative Adversarial Networks* (GANs) (https://arxiv.org/pdf/1406.2661.pdf). A GAN consists of two networks: the generator and discriminator, which compete with each other in some sense. This constant competition leads to improving the capabilities of the two. Generative adversarial networks can generate new patterns, including, for example, photorealistic images and even videos.

Deep neural networks can be also employed in reinforcement learning. In deep reinforcement learning, convolutional networks are usually used. The input of such systems is the image of the state of a virtual or real world. The output is the set of different possible actions which the agent can take to achieve its reword. The neural network approximates a complicated function that computes which action to take. There are also architectures where two convolutional networks work in consortium with each other.

In addition to convolutional networks, other types of deep ANNs are also successfully used in deep reinforcement learning. For instance, by using recurrent nets, deep reinforcement learning can be much more efficient for some tasks. Some of such tasks require memorization of previous states of an agent, which refers to so-called non-Markovian reinforcement learning.

A recent and interesting approach in deep reinforcement learning is so-called *progressive neural networks* (https://arxiv.org/abs/1606.04671). This approach has been developed by researchers from DeepMind. Progressive neural networks can be used for reinforcement learning, for instance, in robotics. As the researchers say this approach is an important step to building artificial general intelligence because a progressive neural network can learn how to perform a whole series of different tasks, as opposed to other types of ANNs. These networks can be also used in supervised learning.

A progressive neural net represents a combination of several linked-up deep networks, which are called columns. In a progressive network, each column is trained for performing only one specific task. A column that is being trained can use some information from previously trained columns; moreover, the previously trained columns do not rewrite their weights in this process. However, there are certain drawbacks to this approach. The more columns in a progressive neural network, the harder this network learns new tasks. So, these networks are weakly scalable, at least now.

One of the greatest achievements of deep reinforcement learning in recent years was the computer program AlphaGo which won the board game Go, playing against the reigning human world champion. However, this program also uses Monte Carlo Tree Search in addition to deep learning.

In most practical applications, modern artificial neural networks have several hidden layers. Advanced state-of-the-art convolutional deep neural networks have hundreds of hidden layers and hundreds of millions or even billions of adjustable parameters in them. Today's recurrent neural networks are much shallower than convolutional nets. The most powerful recurrent neural networks have only several layers. For example, reportedly, the neural network that is being used in Google Translate has eight layers. The trend is that deep neural networks are getting deeper i.e. with more hidden layers.

It is not clear yet how powerful an artificial neural network must be to acquire human-level intelligence. There is a hypothesis that an artificial neural network with 100 hidden layers can do anything that a human can do in 1 second because natural neurons in the brain fire 100 times a second. But it is most likely an oversimplified view.

Currently, if given the right dataset to train on, deep learning is capable of performing most tasks that humans can do rapidly, usually in less than 1 second (there are some exceptions to this rule). One could argue that this is not really true because tasks that require more than a second to accomplish are nothing more than combinations of 1-second tasks. However, some experts in neuroscience believe that, even for 1-second tasks, the biological brain can do much more and in a fundamentally different way than deep learning does today. In many cases, deep learning has been overhyped. At present, tasks that require true human thinking are not tractable for deep learning. Learning and comprehending the world by pure unsupervised observation is currently not tractable for deep learning either.

We should say that all the types of artificial neural networks we have just discussed are in fact quite primitive models of the information processes that occur in the brain. There are a number of critical distinctions between ANNs/computer hardware and the biological brain. Here, I will mention just a few of them. We do not know all these distinctions because we do not fully know how the brain works.

A neuron in ANNs is a gross abstraction to natural neurons in biological brains. Primary logic gates in the brain are molecular, which work in an intrinsically stochastic fashion due to a constant Brownian motion.

In an ANN, all the neurons perform basically the same function. On the contrary, there are multiple types of neurons in the brain, performing different functions. Moreover, there are around 100 different known types of neurotransmitters in the brain, not to mention neurotransmitter acceptors which serve as molecular neural gates. This allows a biological neural network to have different functionality in its different locations.

The neural network in the human brain is much larger than modern ANNs. There are about

10^{11} (around 100 billion) neurons and 10^{15} synapses in the human brain.

Back-propagation is a global algorithm, whereas the brain most likely uses local learning strategies. Under normal conditions, only a small fraction of neurons in the brain are active at the same time.

In ANNs, neurons are connected to other neurons in adjacent layers; whereas, in the brain, neurons are connected not only to their neighbor neurons but also to neurons from distant locations of the brain. Therefore, the topology of ANNs is much simpler than that of the brain and the neocortex in particular.

The learning algorithm in artificial neural networks changes the weights inside of the nets, but it doesn't change the networks' structure. This type of learning framework is partly present in the biological brain: it is synapses strengthening. But the brain has other mechanisms of learning. In an active brain, some new synapses form between different neurons and some synapses die off all the time. That is to say, the structure of the brain is constantly changing. In addition to synapses, some neurons also constantly form and die off in the brain (but this number is quite small under normal conditions).

Also important is that once trained, an artificial neural network is no longer adjusting its weights at the inference stage, whereas the human brain is constantly learning.

Also, artificial neural networks are prone to so-called catastrophic forgetting, which refers to a process when an ANN becomes incapable of executing a previous task after training for a new task. Mainly because of this, each ANN after training is usually able to perform only one task. It is not the case in natural intelligence of course. Learning new tasks does not make us incapable of doing tasks which we were able to perform in the past. Moreover, previous knowledge from previous experiences is helpful for learning new tasks. Arguably, the accumulated knowledge acquired from all previous experiences in our life is applied to each new task we take. Perhaps, progressive artificial neural networks, as well as some other approaches of so-called *transfer learning*, will be an important milestone towards performing multiple tasks by a single ANN.

Neurons in the brain do information processing by sending discrete spikes of electrochemical activity with apparently random timing. It turns out that this seemingly random timing may be important for transmitting information in the brain. Most types of artificial neural networks do not take into account the timing of the signals they are transmitting.

However, there is a generation of artificial neural networks called spiking neural networks (SNNs) that can more realistically simulate the work of the brain. Neurons in spiking neural networks do process and communicate information by the timing of their activities or spikes, which is very similar to what biological neurons do.

A biological neuron receives electrical impulses from other neurons. As a result, the neuron's membrane potential goes up. When the membrane potential reaches a certain value, the neuron spikes and sends an electrical signal to other neurons down the chain. But the membrane potential has the property of gradually decaying with time, so if the neuron does not receive electrical signals with appropriate timing, its membrane potential can't reach the threshold and the neuron does not fire. So, the timing of neurons' signals really matters for biological neural networks.

There are different types of spiking networks, including feed-forward and recurrent ones. Actually, this type of artificial neural network has been known in the ANN research community since the 1950s.

The back-propagation algorithm can be used for training some types of spiking neural networks, but not all of them. As we have seen, even though back-propagation is currently the main workhorse of deep learning, this algorithm has its downsides, and it is especially the case when it comes to training such networks as spiking ones.

For training spiking neural networks, it has been proposed to use an astonishingly simple neurophysiological principle called *spike-timing-dependent plasticity* (STDP): if the pre neuron fires before the post neuron, the connection between these neurons increases and vice versa. This principle is a particular example of the more general Hebb's rule: *cells that fire together, wire together,* which was introduced by the Canadian neuropsychologist Donald Hebb in 1949.

However, having just the STDP algorithm is not enough for training spiking neural nets. Presumably, this algorithm should be used together with evolutionary algorithms, which we'll be discussing in the next chapter.

I should also point out that some analog neuromorphic hardware is currently being developed exclusively for running spiking neural networks. And there already exist some neuromorphic hardware types specifically designed for running advanced spiking neural networks. For example, SpiNNaker (Spiking Neural Network Architecture) is predominantly designed for research purposes – understanding how the brain works. Whereas, IBM's TrueNorth is a commercial project.

Even though SNNs are the most realistic models of the brain known today, they were essentially useless in practical terms for a very long time. The main problem was that there were no efficient algorithms for training such networks. Only relatively recently, the first practical results of using spiking networks have appeared for some problems, mostly for supervised ones. We'll see if these neural networks succeed in achieving great success in the future. But today we don't know it for sure.

We don't yet fully understand how the biological brain works, so we can't use the brain as an exact blueprint for building artificial general intelligence at this moment.

Some experts think that deep learning is a direct road to artificial general intelligence, but others think differently and propose other alternative ideas. As we said, there are some other interesting techniques in artificial intelligence.

For example, there is a very interesting neuro-inspired – or neuro-constrained, as the authors suggest to call it – approach to machine learning, called Hierarchical Temporal Memory (HTM). The idea of Hierarchical temporal memory was introduced by the brilliant American inventor Jeff

Hawkins in his seminal book *On intelligence*. In this book, he proposed the memory-prediction framework theory of the brain. He also founded the company Numenta, which has some commercial products based on Hierarchical temporal memory.

HTM is a computational model of the mammalian neocortex. The neocortex is the region of the brain that is mostly responsible for cognitive capabilities.

HTM does not formally belong to ANNs, but, at its core, it can also be viewed as a special type of artificial neural network. HTM learns on time-based sequences of unlabeled data in real time. HTM utilizes its own unsupervised algorithm for learning, called Temporal Memory (TM). HT is a memory of sequences of patterns in a data stream.

Hierarchical temporal memory uses a technique called sparse distributed representation (SDR). Sparse distributed representation refers to the state, where only a negligible amount – typically less than 2% – of neurons is active at a time. It is very similar to the biological brain.

A very important distinction of HTM from most ANNs is that HTM learns continuously, without a separate stage of training, and this is similar to the brain. There are other important distinctions. In most types of ANNs, neurons can be in two states: active and inactive. As opposed to other types of

ANNs, there are three states of a neuron in hierarchical temporal memory: active, inactive, and predictive.

In the light of recent progress in deep learning, HTM is not a very popular theory now. But in my opinion, this theory is also very interesting and deserves close attention.

As we said, training neural networks is a hard computational problem, and there is a big practical interest in designing ANNs and hardware for them that exploit computational resources more efficiently. In ANNs, both the training and inference stages can be optimized. There are a number of techniques for improving the computational efficiency of artificial neural networks both at software and hardware levels. Interestingly, some techniques seemingly have their analogies in the biological brain. For example, one technique of optimization of computational resources in ANNs is the pruning of synapses: it turns out that some synapses after training can be deleted without losing much quality of the subsequent inference stage. A similar process also widely occurs in the brain. Though, the consequences of synaptic pruning may be more significant in the brain.

Finally, I should say that deep learning can be implemented using the quantum computing paradigm. Maybe the most obvious choice is using quantum annealing because quantum annealing is all about solving high-dimensional optimization problems. In addition, some quantum algorithms other than quantum annealing can be utilized in ANNs in principle. It has been proposed, for instance, that the weight adjustment in artificial neural networks can be done by using Grover's algorithm instead of using classical gradient-based optimization. In this case, the neurons are computationally classical, but the process of the adjustment of the weights in this network is done on a quantum computer using Grover's algorithm. It is believed that such hybrid architecture could have some advantages over an entirely classical one. There are also proposals of using deep neural networks, in which all their components (neurons, the learning algorithm, the cost function, the training data, etc.) are completely quantum (https://arxiv.org/abs/1902.10445).

Building Artificial General Intelligence

Having discussed some essential concepts and techniques in computation and artificial intelligence, in particular, hopefully, we are ready to delve into a discussion on building artificial general intelligence. As we said earlier, we don't have (at least as far as we know) working examples of AGI. However, there are a number of professional and amateur researchers around the world who try to build AGI. From my point of view, different approaches for building artificial general intelligence can be divided into two very broad meta-categories: engineering approaches and evolutionary approaches, though the line between these two meta-categories is fuzzy.

The engineering approaches can be divided further into two separate groups, depending on the number and diversity of the algorithms they use in an attempt to build AGI. The first group favors architectures with very few similar algorithms or even one algorithm, and the second group refers to architectures with several or many diverse algorithms.

A vivid example of the approaches favoring diversity of algorithms is the OpenCog project, founded by the American scientist and entrepreneur Ben Goertzel. The OpenCog architecture includes artificial neural networks, a probabilistic logic engine, evolutionary algorithms as well as other computational components.

In contrast to that, some experts are inclined to believe that a very sparse set of algorithms or computational methods, for example, only using deep neural networks, can be sufficient for building AGI.

Pedro Domingos, a well-known researcher in machine learning, believes that a universal machine learning algorithm can be created. He argues for that in his book *The Master Algorithm*.

It is well known that different areas of the neocortex perform different functions. For example, there is a visual area, auditory area, motor area, and others. It is also known that if certain areas of the cortex have been damaged or completely removed, other areas can to some extent replace the functions of the impaired areas. This leads to the conclusion that the principles of information processing in all regions of the cortex are most likely identical or very similar. This assumption favors the possibility of building AGI using very few algorithms.

Obviously, an intelligent machine has to receive information from the world. In general, the richer the sensory input, the better the understanding of the world the machine can produce. Here, I should say that machines can sense a far richer range of sensory inputs than we can. For example, machines can perceive X-rays, ultraviolet, and ultrasound. This information must be transmitted in a digital form if we work with digital computational devices.

Given the vast complexity of reality, an intelligent machine should have the ability to discard noise and other redundant information in order to process only necessary information. Otherwise, performing learning would be a much computationally expensive process. Of course, in order to get rid of redundant information, the machine has to determine in the first place whether the information is redundant or not.

As we have seen, nothing, including natural intelligence, can precisely simulate reality. Because of this, in order to comprehend the world, we need to generate abstract concepts and operate with them or think, in other words. The process of thinking or reasoning can be considered as adjusting our models of the world.

The idea that there is a hierarchical structure of patterns or models in our mind has been known probably since the discovery of the structure of the neocortex. Individual patterns, which can be words or ideas, represent simpler models from which more complex models can be constructed, and an overall model of the world in our mind consists of all those smaller models. At a physical level, this overall model is an entire neural network in the brain or at least in the cerebral cortex; whereas different areas of the cortex represent different parts of this biological neural network, which are responsible for forming smaller models like individual words or ideas.

But having only such a hierarchical structure is not enough. We have to build such a system that must be flexible enough to generate different kinds of models of reality, including numerous very specific models and also extremely abstract ones, depending on the situation, and these models should be interconnected with each other. In other words, in addition to a vertical hierarchical structure, there should be also an elaborate *horizontal structure*.

Now, it is widely accepted that logical reasoning is not an innate feature of our minds. In fact, we often tend to use analogies rather than logic when we are thinking. This is very similar to operations on vectors, which we mentioned discussing natural language processing in the previous chapter. However, using just standard word embedding techniques for building word vector representations cannot capture word meanings in a similar way to natural intelligence. And it's not just because we cannot define synonyms using standard word embedding techniques. Due to the rapid progress in deep learning, it is likely that there will be a working method of defining synonyms in the very near future. The problem of capturing meaning in a similar way to natural intelligence more corresponds to the fact that when we comprehend the world naturally, we don't derive the meaning of words only by the word context in which they appear. Instead, we use information coming from all our senses and place the meaning of each word in the models of reality in our minds.

However, we need to use logic in order to produce more accurate models of reality. Probably, implicit logic rules, which we use when we think, can be learned by observing the world. And, probably, an unsupervised machine learning system can also *learn* logic this way.

Switching between different sub-models rather than constantly running an overall model of the world is, presumably, the preferable strategy because running an entire model would be a much more computationally expensive approach. There should be some trade-off between running an overall model of the world and smaller sub-models, and the intelligent machine should be able to find such an optimal trade-off. This process is somewhat similar to natural attention. Supposedly, we can use reinforcement learning to get these models to do something useful.

Defining a correct reward function is critically important for building beneficial or at least safe

AGI. In simple terms, AGI should probably make its possessors happy or satisfied. But how happiness or satisfaction can be measured? Perhaps, these ephemeral psychological states can be measured by certain brain activity of the AGI's owners.

The self-awareness of such an artificial intelligence system would be the understanding (sub-model) of its own place in its model of the world.

There are many mathematical techniques for modeling, and neural networks are just one of them. Other very interesting techniques for modeling, which are less known with respect to AI in this day and age, include Probabilistic programming and Cellular automata. But we shouldn't completely ignore the possibility that at this stage we may not even fully have all the mathematical apparatus needed for building AGI.

But let's consider the hypothesis that AGI can be built based on deep learning (It may be terribly wrong of course). From my perspective, in terms of deep learning, our mental activity could be viewed mostly as generative models of our senses and internal representations that are constantly being fed into a reinforcement learning procedure, which apparently has a very complicated reward function. But what are and how do these internal representations form in the first place? The internal representations are just memories and maybe some congenital mental formations. The generative models are induced by memories, but the generative models produce new memories themselves.

It is widely accepted that we have some innate reactions generated by some patterns. For example, scenes with not natural looking or mutilated body parts can provoke horror or repulsion. Conversely, seeing other patterns – for example, such as of a sexual character – can induce unconditional temptation, attraction, or affection. The list of such congenitally predisposed reactions to certain patterns is probably humongous in humans. Moreover, the behavior of some animals and especially insects is largely predisposed or even entirely determined by their innate instincts, and yet these organisms can adapt to an ever-changing and often hostile environment. It is not entirely clear whether such innate reactions are an indispensable component of the highest forms of intelligent behavior. Even if so, we already have direct analogies to examples of innate predispositions in robotics, where some types of robots don't learn really completely from scratch. Some of such innate reactions can be also viewed as a reward function.

The output of the generative models could be also fed into other algorithms, and the input for the generative model could be taken not only from the machine's sensors and associative memory that primarily induce the formation of the models but also from local or global resources of data stored in digital format. In this case, such a system would be capable of performing additional functions.

Imagine an AI system that could generalize as well or even better than we can, instantly access any information on the web or local databases, never get tired or bored, and perform a very big number of specific algorithms. Could such a system be called superintelligence? In my opinion – probably yeas.

Now, let's switch to discussing pure evolutionary approaches to building AGI. The human brain, an amazing thinking device, is a product of biological evolution. The theory of evolution through natural selection is one of the most significant ideas in science ever. This theory was first comprehensively developed by Charles Darwin, whom I refer to as one of the greatest thinkers of all time, with respect to biology in his groundbreaking book "On the Origin of Species by Means of Natural Selection, or the Preservation of Favoured Races in the Struggle for Life" in the middle of the 19 century. Darwin's theory turned biology upside down at the time. However, the theory of evolution by natural selection is relevant not only to biology.

Many natural and especially social processes can be viewed in evolutionary terms. Take for example economy. One reason why a free liberal economy is more efficient than a planned economy is that there are more intrinsic evolutionary mechanisms in a liberal economy. By evolutionary mechanisms in a liberal economy, I mean first of all the natural selection of the fittest enterprises.

Evolution theory, of course, has its place in computer science. In 1975, John Henry Holland published his seminal monograph "Adaptation in Natural and Artificial Systems", where he laid out the foundations of evolutionary computations.

Evolutionary computation is a subcategory of machine learning. There are many diverse and very interesting strategies in the field of evolutionary computation. Probably, the most frequently used strategies include so-called genetic algorithms, which fall under the umbrella of genetic programming.

The three most important principles of evolution – both biological and computational – include heredity, variation, and selection. The general framework of genetic programming is relatively simple. First, we generate a number of solutions to a problem and evaluate for each of them its performance. Then, we create a new generation of the solutions by crossing good solutions with each other from the previous generation, from time to time introducing some random mutations to increase variation. And we repeat this cycle until we have a reasonably appropriate solution to the problem. This process can be very efficiently parallelized, which is very useful in practice. Usually, genetic algorithms find their use when the problem is very complex and there is no need to find the best possible solution to the problem. Genetic algorithms can be used in a humongous amount of domains.

One possible application of genetic algorithms in artificial intelligence is using them as an optimization method in deep neural networks instead of gradient-based approaches. In a broader sense, evolutionary computation is used, for optimizing and building more efficient ANNs that evolve in an evolutionary process.

But evolutionary computation can be potentially used even in a broader domain – for building true AGI. Supposedly, an AGI program can be devised as a product of evolutionary process. However, there are some problems with this approach. First, since intelligence is a very complex phenomenon, we should correctly specify the fitness function for the evolutionary process. Moreover, this fitness function has to be aligned with our goals and values. Second, we should probably set up a proper structure for such an AGI program in the very beginning of the evolutionary process. Otherwise, the evolution may take an unreasonably long time. Third, we would most likely not be able to use simulation because, due to the complexity of our program, simulated environments would be even much more complex and computationally intractable to simulate than the program itself. For this reason, we would most likely need to build a number of physical robotic agents, whose software would represent an evolving AGI program, and place these agents in a real environment. In this case, we again run into another problem: this evolutionary process can take much physical resources and time to evolve such a program. However, probably we don't need a very complicated environment in simulation and a very powerful AGI program to evolve. Maybe we would only need to acquire some crucial component for an AGI program in simulation and then augment this AGI with other functions or just scale it up for the real world.

In order to be able to perform various practical intelligent tasks, computer systems have to acquire an appropriate amount of common human knowledge. I don't think this is a very hard problem especially if we had machines that could learn just by observing the world. Probably, we will soon see the appearance of various new artificial intelligence personal assistants collecting immense amounts of data, including the data about our everyday lives.

A Few Words about Control Problem

There are many concerns about the potential threats that artificial intelligence may someday pose to humanity. Of course, these fears are not totally unreasonable. As with any technology, artificial intelligence requires responsible management and utilization. There have already been examples of artificial intelligence causing some difficulties, for instance, the well-known case of the chat bot which insulted people.

However, the professor of Stanford and chief scientist of Baidu Andrew Ng once very figuratively said about AI threats: "I don't work on preventing AI from turning evil for the same reason that I don't work on combating overpopulation on the planet Mars". Perhaps this statement is too metaphorical, but we can conclude from this quote that artificial general intelligence is currently rather underdeveloped and cannot really hurt people on a massive scale.

When we think about the potential dangers of certain technologies, we should keep in mind that all technologies carry some level of danger, but none of them, including even the most devastating weapons, have wiped out humanity.

Some people, however, consider artificial intelligence as a special technology. Many believe that the creation of artificial general intelligence with capabilities exceeding human intelligence could give rise to serious problems because it would be difficult to supervise this kind of intelligence.

But a human mental structure is not just a pure intellect. Different philosophers used to say much about this, and some of them had even developed their whole philosophical systems around this. Arthur Schopenhauer, for example, describes the world as the will and representation. The representation in Schopenhauer's meaning is similar to what we mean by intelligence. But does artificial intelligence have its own will? The human will comes from inherited instincts such as self-preservation and desire to take pleasure. I believe that the artificial intelligence system that mimics these features can be also developed because our instincts can be represented as some form of information processing. But we don't have to develop such artificial intelligence systems, at least in most cases. We can build smart artificial intelligence without these characteristics. The will of those systems in Schopenhauer's meaning would be the will of the people who operate these systems.

Thank you for purchasing and reading my book! I hope you enjoyed it. You can also consider my other books:

Machine Learning with Clustering: A Visual Guide with Examples in Python

Deep Learning from Scratch: From Basics to Building Real Neural Networks with Keras.

Further reading

Seth Lloyd. Programming the universe: a quantum computer scientist takes on the cosmos, 2006

Scott Aaronson. Quantum Computing since Democritus, 2013

Charles Blilie. The promise and limits of computer modeling, 2007

Leonard A. Smith. Chaos a very short introduction, 2007

Dennis Bray. Wetware: a computer in every living cell, 2009

Richard Jones. Soft machines: nanotechnology and life, 2007

Tony Hey, Gyuri Pápay. The computing universe: a journey through a revolution, 2014

Nick Bostrom. Superintelligence: Paths, Dangers, Strategies, 2014

Ray Kurzweil. How to create a mind: the secret of human thought revealed, 2014

Christof Koch. Consciousness: confessions of a romantic reductionist, 2012

Jeff Hawkins, Sandra Blakeslee. On Intelligence, 2005

Ian Goodfellow, Yoshua Bengio, Aaron Courville. Deep learning (adaptive computation and machine learning series), 2016

Andreas   Wichert.   Principles   of   Quantum   Artificial
Intelligence, 2013

John H. Holland. Adaptation in Natural and Artificial
Systems, 1992

Stuart Russell, Peter Norvig. Artificial Intelligence: A Modern
Approach, 2021

Peter Wittek. Quantum Machine Learning: What Quantum
Computing Means to Data Mining (Elsevier Insights), 2014

Yoav Goldberg   (Author), Graeme Hirst (Editor). Neural
Network Methods for Natural Language Processing, 2017

Max Tegmark. Being Human in the Age of Artificial
Intelligence, 2017

Pedro Domingos. The Master Algorithm: How the Quest for
the Ultimate Learning Machine Will Remake Our World,
2015

Ben Goertzel. AGI Revolution: An Inside View of the Rise of
Artificial General Intelligence, 2016

www.ingramcontent.com/pod-product-compliance
Lightning Source LLC
Chambersburg PA
CBHW071301050326
40690CB00011B/2489